Credits

Editor: **Guy Andrews**
Design: **Jonathan Bacon**
Production Editor: **Sofie Andersen**
Sub Editor: **Chris Campbell**
Marketing and Advertising: **Jon Cannings**
Editor-at-Large: **Camille J McMillan**
Publishers: **Simon Mottram and Bruce Sandell**

Cover photograph: **Ben Ingham**

Contributors to this annual include:
Gerry Badger – Writer, broadcaster and photographer
David Millar – Professional cyclist with the Garmin-Slipstream team
Nando Boers – Journalist with Sportweek
Matt Seaton – Author and editor of Comment is Free at the Guardian
William Fotheringham – Author and cycling correspondent for the Guardian
Graeme Fife – Author, broadcaster and playwright
Herbie Sykes – Author
Jack Thurston – Author and broadcaster
Bill Strickland – Editor of Bicycling magazine
Johnny Green – Author and Rouleur columnist

Special thanks go to: **Edwin Ingram** at **Tapestry**, **Al Tullett** for his driving skills, **Patrick de Loof**, everyone at **Rapha** and to all the race organisers, team managers and riders who allow us to get closer to the sport.

Printed in the UK by **Butler Tanner & Dennis**

Rouleur magazine is published quarterly – ISSN 1752-962X
The Rouleur Annual and the magazine are both published and distributed by Rouleur

Rouleur Limited, 1st Floor, Imperial Works, Perren Street, London, NW5 3ED
WWW.ROULEUR.CC +44 (0)20 7485 5000

© 2009 Rouleur Limited ISBN 978-0-9564233-0-6

Contents

FOREWORD

Gerry Badger

It's not (just) about the bikes: thoughts on photographing cycling

Lance Armstrong's autobiography was famously called It's Not About the Bike, and he was right. The sport of cycling – and, by extension, the art of photographing it – is not just about the bikes. It's about our heroes, to be sure, but also about those who turn out to watch, the accompanying caravan, the towns and villages through which the race passes, the weather and, above all, the landscape. Even being a spectator is not just about the bikes: it's about the camaraderie of waiting for the caravan and then the riders – whoosh, and they're gone – the roadside picnics, the impromptu meetings with strangers, the pâté and cheese and, of course, the wine and beer.

In short, it's a social sport, even down to the words, friendly or otherwise, passed between opponents in the peloton. And as a social sport, it's intimately connected to communities and the terrain. So the photography of cycling is not just sports photography – it's landscape photography, and portrait photography, and social documentary, and everything in between. It's a great sport to photograph because you can concentrate on the race or be much more elliptical and photograph the spectators, the mise en scène – whatever you wish.

I inevitably got into cycling through the Tour de France before moving on to the Giro, the Vuelta and the Classics, and now I'm very passionate about the sport. July is lost to anything else, and what I first liked about the

Tour before I appreciated what was really going on was that it is a journey through France. Of course, the race situation is important, but the decisive moments in a six-hour day can be compressed into, say, 15 minutes. As French TV in particular knows, the rest of the time is a procession through the terrain, a rolling tourist advert, and so those wide-angle helicopter shots are as fascinating as the close-ups from the motorbikes.

The great David Duffield, who drew me more than most into the sport, understood this. Eurosport's legendary Tour de France commentator had his detractors due to his habit of taking his eye off the actual race, but I liked the fact he gave us a torrent of apparently inconsequential facts about the region, about his hotel, about what he and co-commentator Sean Kelly had eaten and drank the previous evening, and so on. For me, his inspired chatter, about nothing and everything, caught the spirit of things, at least from the point of view of both roadside and armchair spectators.

Any sport at a high level isn't easy, and neither is high-level photography of cycling. But unlike many sports, one has a chance, like David Duffield, to be properly discursive. You can get closer to the action than in most sports, but importantly, you can also get further away. You can actually photograph cycling with an old-fashioned large format camera on a tripod (black hood and all), standing a mile away up on the Galibier or Tourmalet and taking in the whole magnificent panorama in great detail.

I once knew a very important collector of photographs, the late Sam Wagstaff, and he told me to forget the pantheon of great photographers in the museum photo collections. Somewhere out there, he said, was an unknown photographer who was great at photographing shoes, or hands, or whatever. They had a direct, passionate connection to what they were photographing, and that's what he looked for. So here's a collection of photographers who are passionate about photographing cycling, which makes them not just terrific cycling photographers, but terrific photographers full stop. Within the whole spectrum of sports photography, cycling photography for me is the most interesting and inventive genre, regardless of my interest in the bikes.

Paris, Tour de France, 2007 (photo: Gerry Badger)

PROLOGUE

David Millar

It's the beginning of November, and the world of racing seems like a faraway place. I haven't touched my bike for more than a month, but I'm edging closer and closer to dusting it off and beginning my 2010 season. It's amazing how, in a month, I can go from being one of the strongest bike riders in the world to apprehensive about setting out for a two-hour ride; at the moment, riding the Tour de France seems about as possible as flying to the moon. For this reason, I can look at these photos with all the more appreciation. Seeing myself with Brad on Alberto's wheel on the Grand Saint Bernard is a bit haunting – the moment I looked at it, I was taken back to that exact moment. Strange.

That's the power of photography – good photography, anyway: it can suck you into that exact moment and let your imagination paint the rest. This book is full of such images: from Juan Antonio Flecha, the hardest Spaniard, to Alberto, the fastest Spaniard; the rough and tumble and, above all, cold world of cyclo-cross; the mountains of March to the mountains of July; the empty roads and patient fans, then the crazy Giro, with the wet descent that I remember so well (look closer at that one and you'll feel the cold and the fear).

The reflections of Flanders – serene images of a brutal race. The life behind the roads of Roubaix captured in a Peter Beard-like tapestry of postcards, and the timeless images of waiting fans followed by the hyperreal images of some of the most epic of bike races. The road graffiti (or should I say art?) which I only

ever see as blurs if I get to see them at all – it's wonderful to finally witness them now in all their glory. The painted Union Flag remains the most beautiful of these photographs, although it's a shame there's no Saltire – that's always my favourite to roll over.

Then there's the day with the fans at Lombardy. The only time I've been a roadside fan at a Classic was this year at Paris-Roubaix. Doug, the owner of our team, was going along and invited me to join him. I was recovering from a broken collarbone so I didn't mind being seen at the side of the road eating a fried ham (no, it wasn't bacon – it was fried ham) with scrambled eggs sandwich that a bus-load of Flemish fans demanded should accompany the Duvel they had given me. The moment was made perfect when the L'Equipe white car pulled in, parked, and promptly removed from the boot bottles of red wine, baguettes and miscellaneous cheeses and meats. They weren't surprised to see me adorned with dripping sandwich and beer, and at one with the Flemish nutters – this, after all, was Paris-Roubaix. That, basically, encapsulates the Classic spectator experience: no matter what you do at the roadside, it is quite average compared to what will be happening on that same piece of road at some point in the near future.

The Classics are remnants of a bygone age, when cycling really was crazy, when the longer, harder and more ridiculous the event the more it was feted by the public. Fans haven't lost their love for the extreme, and of course the cyclists have never stopped loving hurting themselves.

The only difference is that the sport is mildly more humane than it was back then – I say mildly, because just finishing a Classic remains a feat of awesome physical and mental prowess. They've never really been my cup of tea – I think I got scarred so bad doing them in the late '90s that they've left irreparable psychological damage which I will never conquer. That doesn't mean I'm not open to taking part in them – I pick up my Paris-Roubaix bike from the service course next week. After watching the total devastation and the empty shells of men arriving in the Roubaix velodrome I swore to be part of it. Well, that and the drunken pact I made with Martijn Maaskant that I'd be there. Like I said, we love it, and this book of photographs reminds me just why.

Post-Vuelta – Liège mass pile up (photo: Mrs Nicole Millar)

TIMM KÖLLN

TIMM KÖLLN

The way he goes about his business

It was the day of the Tour de France team time trial, and photographer Timm Kölln had set his sights on shooting the cover of my book, In The Tour. That morning, we studied the route through Montpellier in the Tour road book. We made a plan based around Skil-Shimano, the Dutch team that I had come to know inside out. As with most good plans, the idea was simple. First, we would watch the riders prepare in the shade under the trees in front of their team buses. Then, after the first teams set off in front of the opera house, we would jump in Timm's Golf and hit the technically demanding course. Along the way, we would try to stop at two spots – the outskirts of a village called Grabels and somewhere near Lavérune.

Five Skil-Shimano riders would crash heavily that day. Piet Rooijakkers ended up in hospital with a broken arm. Some cried after they passed the finishing line. Their good start to the Tour had taken a knocking, but they would get their act together again and become even more of a team than before. Granted a wildcard entry by the Tour organisers, they came to France as boys who rode bikes and went on to become men in the space of a week.

We had found a small, narrow bridge with concrete barriers, partly under construction with road signs warning of danger. Riders came by at full speed. French cycling fans drinking in a nearby tent climbed up from the valley and stood by the bridge every time a gendarme on a

motorbike passed, and it was my job to kindly ask them to step back a little. Our team was coming and we didn't need beer-swilling French fans on the cover of the book. We needed the riders, their time trial bikes, the concrete and the signposts. ("I love narrow places," said Timm. He hates roundabouts – too wide, he figures.)

They passed, all nine of them still together, and I heard Timm's camera snapping a few times. Then they were gone, and we had to run at full speed back to the Golf parked a couple of hundred metres up the road. In the car, Timm drove with his camera on his knees. He loves to shoot while driving – you can see the results in his shots of Juan Antonio Flecha and the Castilla y León.

We made it in time to Lavérune; sadly, Piet Rooijakkers did not. We had to drive quickly, and to my surprise Timm did just that, throwing our carefully-planned schedule out of the window. He stepped on the gas over the hills to reach the location for the next shot in time – that was all that mattered. He got the shot, but I never saw the result because it didn't pass Timm's exacting standards. This man from Berlin, one of the best photographers in the business, slept in campsites during our trip. He complained a little once in a while, but he loved the project and cycling too much to let it affect his work.

I first met Timm at the 2007 Scheldeprijs while working on a feature about Skil-Shimano for Sportweek magazine. I had watched cycling all my life, but as a reporter I had only written about Formula One, football and baseball.

When I joined Sportweek in 2006, I wanted to cover cycling, and I figured the best way to understand the sport was to get inside a team. And, after a series of talks, I was lucky enough to be more than welcome at Skil-Shimano.

Timm was draping his white sheet against a wall that day in Antwerp as he prepared a shot for The Peloton, his soon-to-be-published series of riders' portraits taken immediately after races. I don't know which rider from Skil he shot at the Scheldeprijs, but from that day people would know Timm was around if they saw that sheet hanging up near the finish line. We ended up collaborating – he had taken photos of his friend Pedro Horrillo, and I had struck up a correspondence with the Spanish rider for a book on his season which will be published in English by Mousehould Press – and now we were working together on a second book.

After the time trial in Montpellier, our focus changed to Kenny van Hummel, the rider who L'Equipe named worst climber in the history of the Tour. I would change that to the climber with the smallest physical motor but the biggest inner strength.

It happened at the end of stage 16 in Bourg-Saint-Maurice. It was to be the last time van Hummel crossed a finish line in the 2009 Tour, although we didn't know it then. We wanted to take a shot of him after the race, a shot that would tell the whole story of the pain, anger and agony, of the love for a sport throughout its hardships. I tapped Kenny on the back after he passed the finish and

told him I needed only 90 seconds of his time.
I've known Kenny quite a while, so he said: "No
problem." I told him to ride straight to the team
bus, get off his bike and just stand there. Nothing
more, nothing less. "Timm is waiting for you," I
said. "And don't wipe your face with a towel."

Like one of Lance Armstrong's bodyguards, I
moved everybody out of the way with Kenny on
his bike behind me after his long and lonely ride
through the Alps. I ran, pushing people politely
but firmly out of the way. As always, there was
mayhem around the bus – kids were walking past
on the pavement, old men and women, mothers
with buggies – but Timm was there, as he said
he would be. He had endured a traffic jam to
make the journey, not knowing what to expect
at the end of it and unsure if the light was good
enough. He had already taken a good shot of
Kenny a couple of days earlier from the car, but
he figures any chance he gets is a good one. So
he lies down on the grass and shoots Kenny and
me. We laughed, we spoke, and Timm did what
he did in a matter of seconds. And it was not the
portrait that pleased him – it was me and Kenny
laughing moments later. Planning is everything,
but so is timing. The best pictures are shot in a
couple of seconds. Just ask Timm Kölln.

Nando Boers

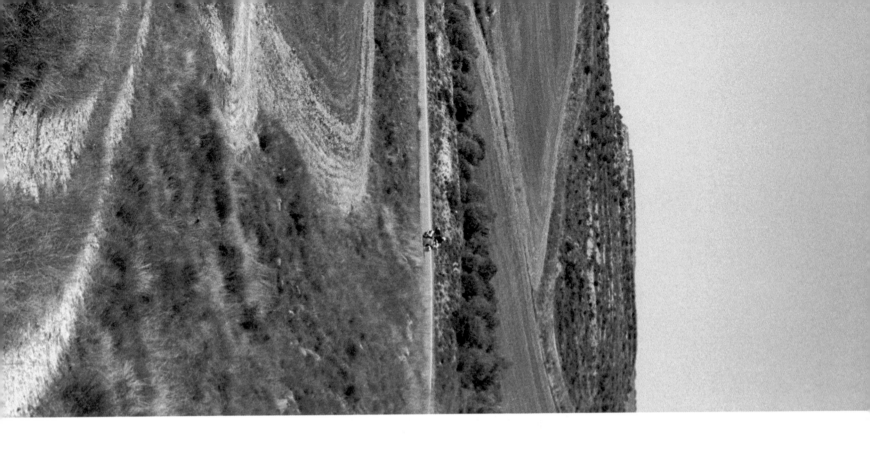

MARTHEIN SMIT

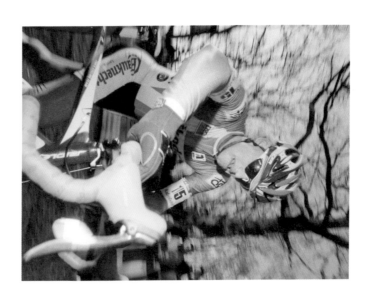

MARTHEIN SMIT

Boom time

In the Low Countries, cyclo-cross is a secular religion. And like any religion, it is riven with the dogmatism and sectarianism of its true believers' differing, divided loyalties. The high priests of cyclo-cross, its stars, claim fanatical devotion from their adherents: in this sacred cause, profanities and even punches are exchanged between the rival congregations of supporters.

Belgium regards itself as the spiritual home of cyclo-cross, and even when the World Cup calendar takes the race venues to Holland and beyond, the Flemish legions make the pilgrimage to follow their champions. Occasionally, some foreign interloper from France, the Netherlands or the Czech Republic arrives to challenge the Belgian orthodoxy, but such heresy rarely takes root. Until now. From the Netherlands a new star has risen, a virtual demigod in this deeply tribal, atavistic world of cyclo-cross. And his name is Lars Boom.

When I think of Lars Boom, I see orange – the orange of his Rabobank squad, the orange of Holland. Orange is also the colour of falling leaves, and oranges are a winter fruit, and at a time when most cyclists go into hibernation, Boom goes to work. Sven Nys versus Bart Wellens, cross's dominant narrative of recent years, has been forced to give way to the young Dutchman's eminence, as Boom has moved seamlessly up from the junior world title through gold in the U23 ranks to capture the 2008 rainbow jersey at Treviso in Italy.

Back home in the Netherlands, he holds a record of national cross champion's titles, unbroken since 2001 when he was 16. For good measure, last year he cleaned up with the Dutch road race and time trial titles as well. When he's not wearing a rainbow skinsuit, he's as likely to be in the national champion's red, white and blue jersey. But I still think of orange.

Again, in contrast to the Wellens-Nys dynasty, Boom breaks the mould of the compact, agile type of crosser. At six feet three inches and weighing 75 kilos, he is more the tall, rangy Erwin Vervecken type – except he's more than a decade younger. Yet far from looking like a roadie who has merely come to terms with a cross bike, he is as fleet of foot and fluent in transitions as the finest.

But he is a roadie, too, and a fine time trialist – a time trialist who can handle a bike, that rare animal. Watch the majestic style in which he won stage 15 in this year's Vuelta, riding for the Rabobank road team. On the final climb of the day, he simply rode his breakaway companions off his wheel with a cruel cadence. He punched it over the top to drop David Herrero, his last hanger-on, and then hurled himself down a narrow, technical descent that saw the Spaniard ride off the road after a couple of curves. Boom had ample time to celebrate when he crossed the line in Cordoba. Awesome orange.

Besides the flair, there's no question that there's a big engine under the Boom bonnet. With those long levers, he can crank out the watts.

Watch him in a world cup race such as last year's Grand Prix Adri van der Poel at Hoogerheide on a really sticky, old-fashioned cross course with sections of ankle-deep mud: Boom just muscles his way through. While the best of the rest struggle to keep a gear turning, Lars looks as though he is riding in a different race. He has that crosser's necessary knack of riding light to apply the power. There's delicacy and finesse to complement his strength. He doesn't need the going to get tough in order to get going. When he took the world title at Treviso, it was a cold, dry day on a hard, fast course.

Several other top cross riders, Nys and Niels Albert among them, maintain respectable road careers, but most make no great departure from the anonymity of the peloton. For them, it is a way of making a living in the off-season; the trails, dunes, ramps and run-ups of the world cup cross scene are where they shine and establish a rep. But Boom is amassing a serious list of road palmarès, topping the general classification in the Tour of Belgium in 2009 and claiming the climber's jersey on stage four of the Vuelta.

Boom is simply the complete rider, a truly achieved all-rounder. Given how far he has come at just 24, and just looking at him – the way he can climb and ride against the clock – you have to ask yourself, is this a possible grand tour winner? And that's not just the armchair directeur sportif talking; he's a marketing executive's dream. If you could genetically engineer a cyclist for the podium, you would end up with something looking a lot like Lars Boom: all blonde hair, sharp cheekbones and a smile full of white teeth.

Mark my words, Boom time is just around the corner. Look beyond the dun winter landscape of Hoogerheide, and the future is orange.

Matt Seaton

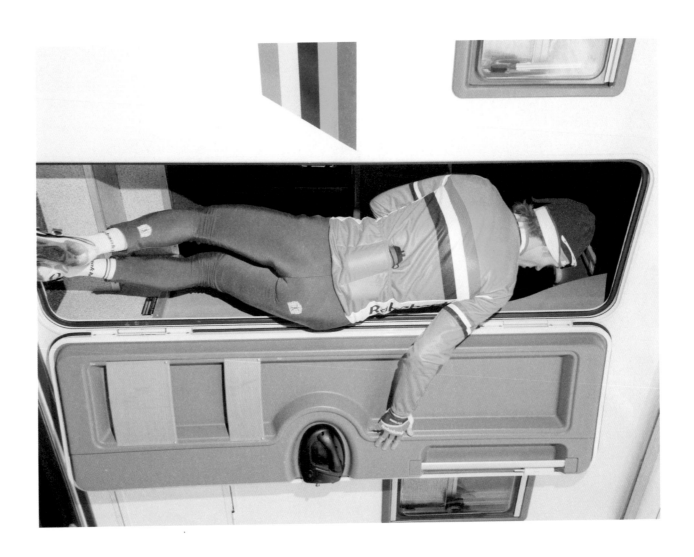

GERARD BROWN

GERARD BROWN

Journalism is a reductive business, so let's be brutally minimalist about the 2009 professional road cycling season. Distil the last 12 months of pro bike racing and you end up with four names: Lance Armstrong, Fabian Cancellara, Mark Cavendish and Alberto Contador. The old Texan, the Swiss on a roll, the talkative fast one and the quiet Spanish one. The best climber, the best sprinter, the best time trialist and the best comeback man. As for 2009's memorable location, that's easy: the obvious candidate is shiny, giant and, according to the structuralist Roland Barthes, has a personality all of its own: bald, capricious, vicious, implacable Mont Ventoux.

The Armstrong-Contador confrontation has all the classic elements of the great cycling duels of the past, with a few little twists of its own: the old gunslinger pulling on his six-shooters for one last duel with the new kid on the block (think Gino Bartali and the younger, stronger and equally unstoppable Fausto Coppi in the post-war years); teammates in the same colours, but divided by a single goal and radically opposed personalities (Coppi and Bartali again, in the Italian jersey, plus Stephen Roche and Roberto Visentini in the blue, red and white of Carrera in 1987); and psychological warfare, with the older man using his experience to goad the younger man (shades of Jacques Anquetil and Raymond Poulidor through the early '60s, or Bernard Hinault and Greg LeMond in the mid-'80s).

Cavendish is in a different class, so too is Cancellara. If Armstrong and Contador offer

an element of soap opera to pep up what they have to offer on the road, the year's best sprinter and the top time trialist ooze sheer supremacy in their chosen field. It would be possible, if not exactly likely, for Cavendish to say nothing and his results could speak for him and his team. Which is why Gerard Brown's pictures here get it right: Cav's wins are a collective effort, summed up by the images of the Manxman behind his yellow and white troops, or alongside George Hincapie on a podium. (Hincapie, lest we forget, played a key role in the final kilometres of Milan-San Remo, helping to set up Britain's first win in a cycling Monument since the 1960s.)

As for Cancellara, his total dominance of the time trial at the worlds in Mendrisio summed up several years in which he has been to the *contre-la-montre* what Cav is to the sprint and Contador is to the high mountains. Each is master of his domain, as peerless as an Eddy Merckx, but not as polyvalent.

A personal note here: my racing moment of the year, and it has come in from left field, is Cancellara descending in the Alps during stage seven of the Tour de France to regain the peloton twice due to two wheel changes. Captured by television motorbikes as he swept from bumper to bumper, missing team cars by inches, it was bike riding turned into art, breathtaking in the confidence and perfect coordination of man and machine in an environment that offered new challenges every second.

There's a fifth name to throw into the 2009 mix, and not just if you are British: Bradley Wiggins, the newcomer at the high table of the Tour. His approach can be summed up in one delightful YouTube clip in which he tells a television interviewer that he's just going to get up and eat his Weetabix and get on with it. To hell with mumbo jumbo – as Sean Yates would say, just ride your bike.

It's easy to boil down a pro cycling season to a list of names and places, but one of the joys of sport is that certain elements are universal, whether you are riding the Wannabee Wheelers' Fish and Chipper or the Tour – or, in the case of Gerard's pictures, the Tour du Vaucluse, a lesser event with a worthy history all of its own, or the Tour of Switzerland, a decent foil to the Big Three grand tours.

The road surface, be it cobbles that shake your innards or just the worst efforts of the local council with chippings and tar; the elements, be it the snowdrifts on a high Alpine pass, the crosswind that Armstrong sensed as the moment came to remind Contador who was the oldest and wisest man in the Tour, or the rain, dark and chill of a British winter that instils cold and wet in the very heart of the thickest synthetic shammy inset.

That moment when the break goes, and the guy who has made the move happens to turn around to assess the gap as his fellows gasp for air. A sprint finish, lost and won. The solitude of a high-speed descent; the constant calculations, conscious or instinctive, as the road throws up hairpins, dodgy surfaces, and your fellow cyclists move when and where you don't expect them to. The instant when everything goes horribly wrong and you end up down and out in the ditch, literally or metaphorically.

And we know, in our hearts, that 2010 can be distilled as well. The storylines that will run and run for the next 12 months have been written already: who will emerge the winner when Contador and Armstrong resume their relationship of mutually assured detestation? What will Cancellara and Cavendish achieve next? How will the "Twig" be affected by cycling's biggest transfer battle since the days of Bernard Tapie 25 years ago, and what inter-team politics will result? We can't predict the battleground, but we can hazard a guess or two...

William Fotheringham

OLAF UNVERZART

OLAF UNVERZART

Theatre: Greek *"theatron"*, a place for seeing, from a verb which means "to gaze at, behold". Does an empty theatre have any point? There is little to see: a vacant stage, unoccupied seats, bare boards, the curtains drawn to either side of the open space. It craves a drama to give it purpose, to fulfil its function, to breathe life into its hollow "O".

And what of these empty roads, the flanking woods, this pattern of stone mosaic, pieced together by Flemish artisans nurtured in the skill, months on hands and knees, plating the bare earth over ground where the Roman legions had once laid their military roads to bring war, law and taxes? Every one of these paved ribbons across the flatlands of Flanders has brought much of all three, the components of strife laid on one people (the weaker) by another (the stronger). Belgium, trampled down by endless successions of conquering hobnails. Except that when Julius Caesar, first of the rampaging thugs, encountered the local Belgae, he was so shaken by their ferocity that he declared them fiercest of all the Gallic tribes. They were subdued but forever troublesome. And this is their theatre, these highways of unyielding pavé. There isn't one stretch of hill or flat that cannot echo, by name, the pantheon of stars who have turned in stunning acts of dramatic brilliance on them, magical metamorphoses from mere mortals into gods, bestriding the podium like a colossus through whose legs peep the men whose own star turn was just to get to the finish line. The extras? The walk-ons? No. This theatre has room only

for the cast of equals, the men strong enough to ride at all, to appear on these roads of the great Flemish amphitheatre.

The epic spectacle played out in the round to an audience of thousands – that's what these roads are waiting for. It is impossible to look at them without knowing that this is what will give them their true life, their transient glory. It is also impossible not to see, behind their vacancy, underlying the apparent calm in the silence, the racket of all pandemonium let loose. The camera on long exposure captures the tension in that expectancy, staring down the empty road.

The Roman historian Tacitus denounced the notion of an empire and its masters. "They create a desolation," he wrote, "and call it peace." Once, there were countless stone yards and stone pits across Flanders served by men wielding hammers, cold chisels and sizing frames, fashioning endless heaps of cobbles to make causeways impervious to the endless driving rain which constantly saturated, often flooded, the land to either side, rendering it impassable. The only way to traverse these stone streets of ancient date is to pursue the one fame that counts above all with the modern Belgae: victory in their races, Ronde van Vlaanderen, Liège-Bastogne-Liège, Gent-Wevelgem, Flèche Wallonne.

The people without mountains located their gods in forests. Gaze into the depth of the trees where spirits stalk them and lurk.

The people with mountains, on the other hand… the Bald Mountain, for instance. Mont Ventoux. The baldness has a perfectly rational explanation. The region out of which it rears like a volcanic plug of solidified ash originally lay under a vast, though relatively shallow, tropical sea. A submerged coral reef evolved, teeming with animal life. The debris of crustacean shells together with detritus falling into the sea from the land above the waters accumulated on the seabed, solidified, and formed an imposing massif of hard, white rock, the calcareous stone which adorned the mountain relief of the Vaucluse when the waters receded. Which may also explain the presence of a couple of plastic inflatable sharks on the bone-white scree. As to a herd of sheep contemplating the same bone-white scree and perhaps, in the shallow fogs of the ovine brain, concluding that this may be an ossuary containing the remains of their ancestors, I leave that to the osteopaths.

Up there, though, it's… up there. There's no getting away from it. It's very far from rational, logical. You don't have to believe in any of the Mystic Meg stuff, or gods or fairies, to sympathise with the people who lived at the foot of Ventoux, aeons past, and, hearing the terrible winds howling round its bleached peak, thought: "Got to be something going on up there." Put primitive superstition into the mix and figure the added risk the first men who ventured up there knew they were taking: natural calamity with the chance of divine wrath on top. Very much on top.

There is a sort of sub-Olympian hierarchy connected with Ventoux, of course: your Gauls housing their man up there, your Goths supplanting him with one of theirs, your Christians supplanting both with theirs — eternal, almighty everywhere-at-once and universal for good measure, to obviate any future pagan dispossession. They did not bank on the Tour de France, of course, the demigods on bikes, an entirely new possession of the sacred heights. Not that the winds of the Gaulish god ever went away, either: he is sturdier than any bell, book and candle, more elusive than mere faith, more permanent than the vapours of incense. He is also quick to reassert proprietary rights on his old seat, in tandem with those other mischiefs of the Ventoux: Sol, god of the open-cast furnace, and Mistral, goddess of the screaming gale.

And the Tour comes up and sometimes over, and the crowds gather on the barren, sun-flayed slopes. Waiting, they stare out at the nothingness, caught in a haze of heat like a bunch of Seventh-Day Adventists who have read the scripture (or back copies of The Wizard, or whatever it is that they consult), gathered in expectation of Götterdämmerung or Judgement Day or the second coming of Michael Jackson, or whatever. But maybe that's only a trick of the apocalyptic light. On deeper investigation, they are fans – that's what they are, fans investing another sort of vacancy, the summit emptiness of the big mountain on whose own stone causeway stand the motorhomes, the baggage train of the army of spectators waiting for the action, waiting for this petrified open-air arena to resound with the next act in the annual drama. Ventoux. Not like any other mountain. Takes orders from no one. Be careful. Action…

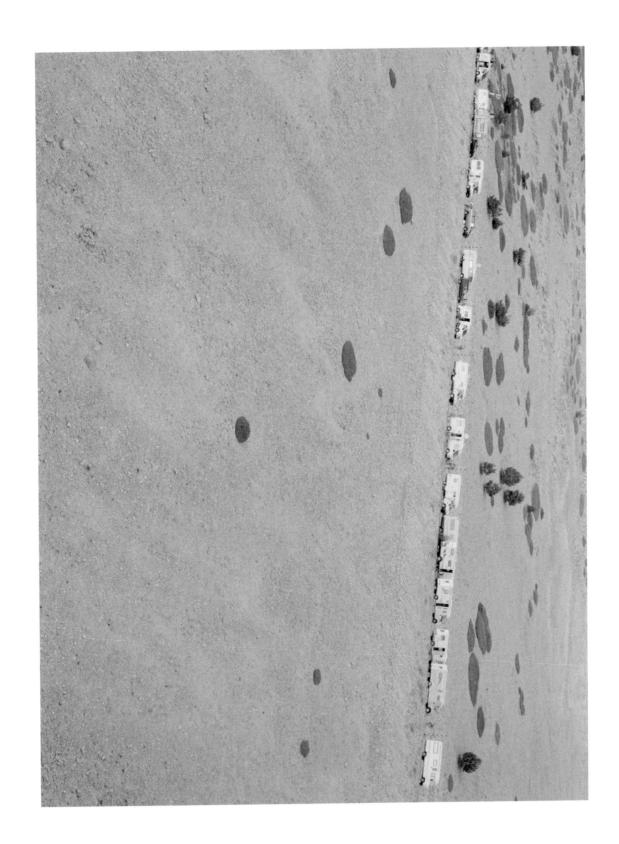

DANIEL SHARP

The centenary Giro d'Italia, then, that of 2009. How best to celebrate a century of timeless, magical split seconds, those upon which Italian cycling was built? How to pay homage to the pink of a hundred early summers? How to honour implacable peoples, extraordinary landscapes, the ebb and flow of a new country which venerates ancient values, age-old traditions? How should we celebrate cycle racing's extraordinary achievements? How should we invoke Alfredo Binda and Costante Girardengo, Fausto Coppi and Gino Bartali, Charly Gaul, Eddy Merckx, Gastone Nencini? And how might we remember those in their wake, the countless cycling nobodies who, lest we forget, enabled them to become who they were?

What of the lunacy that compelled them, in 1914, to carry their bikes up the mule track road to Sestriere in a snowstorm? Of cycling's first superstar, Giovanni Gerbi, a Giro finisher aged 47? Or Learco Guerra, so good Mussolini dubbed him "The Human Locomotive" when he pulled on the first-ever *maglia rosa* in 1931? The mythical Cuneo to Pinerolo stage of 1949, the greatest day in the history of cycle sport as Coppi, symbol of the new Italy, became, for eternity, "l'uomo solo al comando" – the man alone in command. Then the beautiful Hugo Koblet, the first non-Italian winner, double-crossed by Coppi on the giant Stelvio at the astonishing Giro of 1953. What of the 1956 edition, won by a weedy, nine-stone former slaughterman named Gaul? He, the

archetypal cycling scrag-end, was so blitzed with amphetamine that he forgot he was riding – into immortality – through a blizzard over five Dolomite monsters wearing barely more than a T-shirt and a handkerchief. Four years later, Imerio Massignan, the greatest loser in the history of the race and an idol still to millions of Italians, invented the legend of the Gavia, re-invoked by the courageous young American Andy Hampsten some 28 years later. The brilliant, fragile Italo Zilioli, so terrified to win in the mid-'60s that he finished second behind three different victors without spending a single day in pink. Or the day at the 51st Giro, that of 1968, when a young Belgian cyclist smashed his way up the Dolomite giant Tre Cime di Lavaredo and reconfigured the cycling paradigm. It was the day that he, Eddy Merckx, and the sport became something entirely other. Cycling became nought but he and his Merckxism, the most persuasive ideology in the history of sport. Then the pantomime act that was Francesco Moser versus Giuseppe Saronni, followed by the 1987 edition, when a brilliant, furtive Irishman named Stephen Roche outraged an entire nation by committing the perfect cycling crime. In 1994, a big-eared, half-bred cycling Messiah called Marco Pantani floated up the 12-kilometre wall that is Passo Mortirolo, inscribing himself, and it, into the legend of the *corsa rosa*. What of these, and of Carlo Galetti's stealth, Fiorenzo Magni's insatiable thirst for battle? What of Franco Balmamion's indomitable spirit, Giovanni Brunero's climbing genius? And

what of poor, desperate Orfeo Ponzin, killed, like Juan Manuel Santisteban and Emilio Ravasio, chasing the Giro's rainbows?

What of them? The centenary Giro d'Italia somehow contrived to forget them all, to ignore the 99 that conceived it. It failed, inexplicably, to locate Calabria, Sicily, Apulia, Aosta. Though it barely touched the Alps, it dithered its gormless way, presumably by accident, into Switzerland, wasted two stage finishes in (of all places) Austria. The race somehow forgot Massignan's Gavia, Merckx's Tre Cime. It bypassed Bartali's Passo Rolle, Coppi's Pordoi, Stelvio and Izoard. Worse still it unforgivably defiled Coppi's memory in producing a mongrel of Cuneo-Pinerolo, curtailed, so they would have us believe, because of difficulties related to "communication".

Angelo Zomegnan, Italian cycling's Captain Mainwaring, chose to overlook all the people and places upon which the legend was built. Instead he paid fatuous, cringing homage to Lance Armstrong, the seven-time winner of the Tour De France, whored the Giro to a man out on a training ride. In so doing, and in his arrogance and hubris, Zomegnan shamed 100 years of cycling and cyclists themselves. Worse still, the race shamed its public, those to whom the event truly belongs. The centenary edition saw the lowest viewing figures for 30 years, despite being massively hyped. Is it any coincidence that the last decent Giro, that of 2005, was overseen by Zomegnan's predecessor, Carmine Castellano?

Somehow the 100th Giro failed to be the Giro, failed to be a source of pride, a celebration of what is good about this sport and the country. Visiting its public theatre, fans were at best incredulous, in large measure indignant, in many instances incandescent. Though many argue, with no little reason, that the centenary Giro was the saddest in the history of the race, the fact that they continue to argue, and the force with which they do so, speaks volumes.

Be assured that, come what may, the Giro will survive; it is too important and too wonderful a thing not to. Thankfully, Italy's faith, though severely strained, is so deeply rooted that by now it is intractable, genetically imprinted. Italy, and the Italians, still care deeply about their race. Daniel Sharp's brilliant, insightful imagery bears eloquent testimony to this. He says: "I saw it in the faces of the tifosi at the Blockhaus, in the handwritten signs, the flags, the families brought together. I was looking for the humanity which underpins the Giro, and I found it."

All back next May, and the May after. All back for as long as it takes...

Herbie Sykes

CAMILLE J McMILLAN

CAMILLE J McMILLAN

Count to ten and it's all over. Count to ten in Flemish and any sign that it ever happened will be gone before you remember the word for "four". Such is the transient nature of road racing: the long wait, the brief exhilaration and then that slight disappointment, occasionally followed by hope when you realise that only half the peloton went past and the other half is still to come. So there you are all day, in Flanders with the Flemish, waiting for your glimpse of the peloton with very little but the beer and the land and the Flemish lions to consider. You might expect to see poppies in these Flanders fields, but it's not the season.

I have seen plenty of poppies in places that aren't Flanders, in places where battles were fought long ago, in places where you can still see where the shells fell in 1917. These things don't spring to mind quite so easily when you're standing by the side of the road somewhere in western Belgium, in not-quite-breathless anticipation of an entirely different kind of platoon inching its way towards glory. It's a good thing they've got so much beer in Flanders; all that waiting and the legacy of remembrance might make you prone to melancholy otherwise. There's plenty to say about Flanders, of course, that isn't about waiting and remembering, but that sort of thing gets increasingly difficult to focus on when you've had more than two of those Belgian beers.

Let's see, then: there are cobblestones in Flanders, and short, steep climbs, and rumour has it that it rains sometimes and the wind can be cruel.

Stories about Flanders – and there are plenty of them – are stories about the land, which is what most history is ultimately about. Road racing is a lesser, yet more glorious, form of history, and the sport is also all about the land: those interminable roads that provide its shape and challenge the riders while making it accessible for the fans. You'd think that the Romans, great builders of roads and never ones to deny that a little bit of suffering is necessary, would have appreciated road racing. Aren't most of us descended from Roman legionnaires anyway?

Whatever the case, they've got this race in Flanders, once only a small part of a Roman province called Gallia Belgica. I'm sure you've heard about this race. It's a big event, one of those tours, even though you don't need three weeks to tie all of Flanders together like you do with France or Italy. You just get a day, usually a miserable day, of early, northern spring, just close enough to the North Sea that it really hurts. And whenever photographers go to this race, they take pictures of cobbles and grime and Flemish lions.

Except for Camille J McMillan. Camille took pictures of the riders and the bikes and the sky. He caught the peloton and nothing but in that short space of time it takes to count to ten in any given language. Here they are: the riders, reflected once, in the camera, twice, in the mirror, and three times, in some secret Photoshop tool, until it becomes a Rorschach test of cycling in the shape of a butterfly – like one of those cleverly symmetrical blots of

ink that helpful psychologists use to make you tell them what you see and who you are. And I don't know what it means – but it's a Rorschach so it must mean something, because those are the rules of these kinds of pictures, even if it is just a fanciful trick of simple and advanced technologies. This is certainly how you would see these riders through a glass, darkly – without the road or the land or anything but their bikes and the sky above them. You might argue that's all they need, but it isn't all there is to it. And all those other things are still in there because we know they are.

There's no such thing as purity in this day and age. Everything has a context, and De Ronde has got plenty. It's got history coming out of its ears. See, I may remember little more of this year's edition than Stijn Devolder's rude salute upon winning his second Ronde in a row, but I do remember afternoons of listening to Jørgen Leth waxing poetic (as he did in those early days of cycling broadcasts on Danish television), and nobody waxes poetic quite like Jørgen Leth, about the history – oh, the history – and the Flanders fields. There probably isn't much history in the cipher that is an inkblot on a piece of paper, but therein lies the rub, doesn't it? In Flanders fields, you bring the history with you.

Sofie Andersen

REIN VAN DE WOUW

REIN VAN DE WOUW

Standing on the roadside is not a particularly good place to watch a bicycle race. If, during the long wait, you manage to glean anything about what is happening further up the course, it will be a tangle of contradictions, Chinese whispers passed down the line. Before very long you will stop trying as it gently dawns on you that, like everyone else, you are not here to watch a bicycle race; you are here for the Tour de France.

You wait and wait and eventually the police outriders flash past. Then comes the red car of the lead marshal and shortly after come the first riders in a flood of colour, a singular whoosh of carbon, hard rubber singing on the tarmac. Together, the motion of the pack is smooth and swift, efficient and economical, in contrast with the noisy rabble of service cars that gracelessly bump along in the wake of the peloton. And as suddenly as they came, they are gone. It is quiet once again. The crowd is released from the thrill of the moment. The crowd of which you were a part as you strained for a better view, the crowd of young and old and every age in between, whose faces became familiar in the hours of waiting, that cheered and hollered, the crowd that clapped its hands and beat together long inflatable batons, the crowd that assembled so slowly over so many hours dissolves in just a few minutes. Yes, you have seen the Tour but you are almost certainly none the wiser when it comes to what is going on in the bicycle race.

The best views are not those seen by the millions who line the route each July, picnicking in fields, leaning on the temporary guard rails,

lounging on the curb. The best views are on television. In just two dimensions a fabulous tapestry is uncovered, obtained from the most extraordinary and bewildering vantage points. With an eye in the sky, we see the peloton strung out and snaking around traffic islands, through villages, in and out of long avenues of trees. Like mechanical rabbits looking back at the chasing dogs, the motorcycle cameramen render *la tête de la course* in an unreal reverse angle. It is an unremitting gaze that peers into eyes and mouths, recording every breath, every minute gesture, allowing us to study the riders in anatomical detail, the muscular pistons beating out a crazy rhythm which drives them onwards towards the finishing line. But since the cameras maintain a constant distance to the riders, their impressive speed over the ground is quite imperceptible. Telephoto lenses compress space and diminish the gaps that required such huge effort to open and will require still greater effort to close. To know the speed of the peloton and the gaps between the riders, we must wait for the information to be displayed in digital read-out on the screen. We may know more, but we experience less.

Modern television's panoptical feast is, of course, a carefully composed hyper-reality and is quite in keeping with a long tradition of Tour reportage. In the days before live radio and television, when print was king, journalists would go far beyond artistic license in rendering their accounts of the day's racing. After all, the Tour was devised as a way of selling newspapers, and Henri Desgrange, its

original patron, was not a man to allow the truth to get in the way of a good story. With the express instructions of Desgrange, actions and events were deliberately misinterpreted, and the rules of the race were bent, broken and remade – always in the interests of serving up just the right blend of drama, heroic endeavour and fraternal self-sacrifice.

The sheer scale of the event and the powerful complicity between the race and the media serves to maintain the great paradox of the Tour: see it with your own eyes from the side of the road and you see little; see it on television and in print, mediated though the eyes of others, and you see everything, but you are consuming a highly manufactured narrative. This year's Tour marked the return of Lance Armstrong, among the greatest of the Tour's storytellers, seeking to add another chapter to his own epic. It is said that history is written by the victors and Armstrong has always ensured his own account of events becomes the official version. Pedal Pusher, a new stage play that was performed in London over the summer, delves deep into the events, real and imagined, of the Armstrong era. One of its most illuminating moments is when the fictional Jan Ullrich implores: "Tell me what you saw, not what Armstrong told you you saw!"

These photographs by Rein Van De Wouw offer an unusually unvarnished view of bicycle racing. They record what happens in a town, a village, a quiet country road, when one of the really big races passes through. In the series of images from Paris-Roubaix, a race which, unlike the

Tour, follows a very similar route each year, Van De Wouw is drawn less to the manufactured heroics of the race itself than to the intimate side of the spectacle. He is introducing us to the people for whom the race is an old friend, an annual ritual that marks the passage of time or for the young something that sparks dreams of the future. Turning his photographs into a series of postcards to a friend for whom the appeal of Paris-Roubaix is a mystery, Van De Wouw comes clean and admits that, for him at least, the notion of the photographer as a dispassionate observer is a fabrication. He is glad to be standing on the roadside, one of the crowd, straining for a better view.

Jack Thurston

Beautiful people, just here in this deserted country. Esmerald films
the riders who train on the course the week before 'Roubaix'.
At least that's what she tries to do. I saw her there a couple of times. But
every time she was just too late. Or her
mother was standing in her sight.

Well, she couldn't car less.
Esmeralda had just
too much fun over
there.
You should have
seen her!

Esmeralda and her mother.

← le pavé d'arenbers

Wim Luijkx
Aurelia 33
4814 VM Breda
Holland

She also brought a sound technician. You should have seen him! What a guy!
He wasn't a racing cyclist by the way. But he followed Esmeralda, with his rod, dressed
in his racing suit with tight short he ran after her!

I see you're thinking. You think. And think.
You think three men. Three men and a machine.
What are they doing over there?

I'll tell you.
Those guys
are digging
a hole.
Not just a
hole, oh no,
a special
hole.
In that
hole a pole
will be
placed,
against that hole a solid fence. A solid fence for the fans to stand
behind one would you think. But no, this time it's different.
A big fence for the riders so they don't go behind it. Strange isn't it?
I see you're thinking. Well I didn't make it up either.

The riders are riding their bikes on such a bloody bad road that they try to find their way next to it. In the sand. But it's not allowed anymore. They have to fall and suffer!

Drive des Boules d'Hain.

Wim Luijkx
Ancelia 33
4814 VM Breda
Holland

NEDERLAND €0,44

Wallers, where women rule

Wim Luijkx
Aurelia 33
4814 VM Breda
Holland

814VM 33

And then that boy.
In the mornty I saw him viding his bike. fanatically curved forward over his
bend handle bars. He took a right turn just behind the mines and I lost him.
That morning my thoughts are with him. that boy and his bike.

that afternoon
I saw him
again. All at
once he rode
in front of me.
waving at all
people he knew
and a blown
kiss for a
single handsome
lady.

Wim Luijkx
aurelia 33
4814 VM Breda
Holland

As I ride next to him and ask him for his destiny he can't answer. He simply didn't
In secret I already knew. On a way to nowhere!   know.
all at once his hands grip the lower part of the handlebars. He Breaks away!
"paris - Roubaix" He shouts out loud. He stamps on the pedals. Obviously
too high a gear. That afternoon we raced!

had a bad today...

I as if a cobblestone is replaceable.
didn't sleep well that night.

Wim Luijkx
Aurelia 33
4814 VM Breda
Holland

HOSv 4814VM 33

All prepared for race-day

Wim Luijkx
aurelia 33
4814 VM Breda
Holland

TAZ DARLING

TAZ DARLING

One of my favourite ways of demonstrating how bicycle racing is like jazz is to propose that the spaces between the notes are as important as the notes themselves; everyone from Bill Evans to Tom Boonen has shown this to be the case. More often than any reasonable person could predict, what happens between what happens is what is really happening. That's the photography of Taz Darling.

I like traditional race photography. I want to see the iconic picture, the decisive move frozen in time that changes everything for all time, the series of shots that tell the story from start to finish, and the rare magical snap that captures the whole race in a single image. I want to see Alberto Contador's face when he waltzes away from everyone on Verbier. (Hell, I want to see Lance Armstrong's face when Contador waltzes away from everyone on Verbier.) But there is plenty of that around, plenty of great shooters to give it to us, and plenty of places for us to get it.

What Taz shows us is something harder to find, something more fragile and more personal. In her work there is none of the automatic majesty, the power to endure in our communal consciousness, that is granted to the photographs of the crucial moments. There is nothing in Taz's work to create permanence and poignancy but the composition and our own understanding of what we are looking at. She's shooting the spaces, and it's my belief that you can't fully interpret or appreciate a bike race without respect for the potency of those moments.

Back in 2005, I was basting my lungs in carbon dioxide during an open criterium – an unlikely and uncommon event that sees aspirants such as myself line up with pros, including national and world champions – when a massive slab of a man decided to have an early dig. It was Stefan Steinweg, a three-time track world champion and Olympic gold medallist, and he did not so much attack as rumble off the front one mile per hour faster than the group, then 2mph faster in a few more pedal strokes, then three, then four and five and six, and on up to a speed that crumpled the legs of the few optimistic chasers as surely as if he were smashing their knees with a crowbar.

By the time the other stars of the pack got themselves scared enough and angry enough and chagrined enough to get organised, Steinweg had maybe a football field's lead. I sat myself close enough to the fire to get singed but not incinerated, the absolute front of the middle, and for the first few minutes I watched Steinweg simply keep riding away from a rotating paceline that included another Olympic gold medalist, at least two national champions, five or six pros and a couple of hotshot juniors. I was pretty sure that not only was the pack not going to catch Steinweg but that, on a one-mile course, he was going to lap us. Then the chase started blowing up, flinging its weak out to the sides where they flailed in misery as we streamed past, and the whole race went single-file. Simply to survive, I shrunk my entire awareness to three thoughts: stay on the wheel, get to the next wheel, and pedal circles.

Now stay on the wheel. Pedal circles – you *must* pedal circles. Get to that goddamn wheel. Stay on the wheel. And the wheels became those of riders who exceeded me in skill, class, potential, genetics, training. Over and over and over, those three notes drumming through my head, primitive and pounding, allowed me to hang on way past the point at which I belonged anymore.

Stay on the wheel.

I remember what happened next as a stillness, but it could not have been so. The wind was screaming with our velocity, and our chains were humming and our wheels were keening and we ourselves were heaving great loud breaths out onto the course. But there was a space between the notes that the race had imposed on me, and without knowing why or what I was doing, I cocked my head as if to listen to the space. I heard nothing.

And that nothing seemed to mean everything, so I rose from the saddle and slashed out to the side and dumped my chain all the way down the cassette and pulled at my pedals as if I was trying to upend my bike. By the time I popped out ahead of the pack, I was going at my max, my full speed, the fullest speed I ever could attain under my own power, and just as I went clear, Steinweg went by me in a whooshing blur. He had lapped us and ridden right through the group, and somehow I'd known it.

His training partner had grabbed his wheel, a six-day racer named Chris Grasmann, and they were gone past me, unreachable, but I was also gone and past, unreachable by the pack, and to my astonishment there was the line we had all been riding for. I rolled over it to complete what must be the weirdest top three in cycling history:

1. Steinweg (three world championships, one Olympic gold medal)
2. Grasmann (six-day racer with multiple victories in Europe)
3. Strickland (once won a coupon for a free cheeseburger)

That's what the judges saw, and my wife and a friend or two, plus the few spectators who might have recognised me because I was a local. That's the part they still sometimes ask me about. That's the moment that would have showed up in a photograph: the space was where it happened.

Taz's picture of Mark Cavendish between the race and the podium. The name of the brothel on the route of Het Nieuwsblad. The Tom and Jerry cartoon playing in an empty spectator's tent at the Forest of Arenberg. The faces, the knuckles, the bearing of the survivors of Paris-Roubaix. Those are the spaces full of meaning and beauty and mystery and joy that make the rest of bike racing matter.

Bill Strickland

GEOFF WAUGH

GEOFF WAUGH

Just Lookin'

The anguished, angelic voice of Roy Orbison floated across the bar: "I close my eyes, then I drift away…" I was staring at this foxy chick while salivating over a slice of citron gateau. We were sitting on the verandah of Chalet Reynard, famed roadhouse for rouleurs, on that sharp dog-leg high on Mont Ventoux, where the trees stop growin' and the tears start flowin'. The screaming heat of late July left us all wilting at the tables. The water tap in the car park barely oozed. I watched a man pedal uphill slowly, determinedly, painfully, on a dodgy mountain bike with a little kid behind in a flimsy trailer. Either I've got a sunstroke hallucination or that bloke's as mad as a badger. The veins in his neck stood out like electrical cables while the young 'un waved a Dutch flag. It figured. I waved back. I could almost hear the breakfast chat: "C'mon, Dirk. Hup, hup. We're gonna have a bike ride up that icky wicky hill."

As a matter of fact, I did have it figured. Come race day for Le Tour, most folk ain't got no access to a swanky restaurant, or a private box, all that celebrity bollocks. No, you jump in the motor, pedal like a maniac, hitchhike or walk. You paint your poverty on the road, proudly, and you eyeball that big-name celebrity rider from the barren roadside. You find yourself hollerin' as if your very life depends upon it. His life is, for sure, on the line – this mountain kills cyclists. There's Tom Simpson, of course, but it very nearly did for Ferdi Kubler and big

Eddy Merckx himself, suckin' on that oxygen mask like Dennis Hopper in Blue Velvet.

That doesn't mean you can't have fun. I'll spell it: F-U-N. Crack out the spray cans. Break out the brushes. It's arty time. There's penance to be done and beauty to be celebrated. (A pal of mine, JB, a painter, reckons that everyone is an artist. Oh yeah? My pictures of hands resemble tennis balls with bananas growing outta them…)

Road graffiti reaches its apotheosis up here in the freeways of the sky. These words on the tarmac are a shout frozen in a moment. There ain't long to read it. It has to be snappy, like a smartass T-shirt, like a swift left jab to the bridge of the nose. It is of no relevance to outline a verse of literary genius from Lord Byron or George Sand. A name is the norm – "I love Lance". Well, *bien sûr,* honey, I know that he loves you too, and sleep easy at night. This takes me back to my youth. "Kilroy was here". I continue to harbour a liking for those child-like emotional outbursts on the walls of dank alleyways: "I fancy Tracey T", "Robin C is gay". Naked expressions for all the world to see.

No other form of text has this clout. Public toilets have long been a fertile breeding ground. I liked the message right above a urinal in Chatham: "Your future is in your own hands."

Flags are de rigueur. The whole idea of a rainbow road, bubblin' up through the sticky surface, is catching on. Forget Banksy 'n'

Jean-Michel Basquiat – this stuff stays where it's laid by ordinary Joes using masking tape and stencil to make 'em slick.

So – and it's a minor wonder – do the riders get to appreciate their namecheck? Promenaders, days later, get to peruse the entire gallery. Cameras in helicopters zoom in for a nanosecond. Maybe it is all done for the gods lookin' down – an evocation of ju-ju, or a contemporary version of the Nazca Lines, those giant spindly creatures traced in the desert skin of Peruvian desert long, long ago. These lines can only be clocked from high in the sky, and hot air balloons had yet to be invented.

I paused by the portrayal of a winged being. It had me reflecting on those poor troubled souls. Willie Nelson, Texan troubadour, sang it right: "Fly on, fly on, past the speed of sound […] angel flying too close to the ground."

Some day, maybe, the burghers of our crazed sport will bow to star pressure, as Armstrong suggested for Alpe d'Huez. Crowds on mountain verges will be contained. The anarchy of passion will be cauterised. Feet shall be removed from the tarmac. No contact with a racing shoulder. No paint sploshed. Perhaps there could be a perspex tunnel from base to summit with the peloton sanitised within. Would this stop the enthusiasm of the street artists? Of course not. What more natural canvas could there be? Check out any underpass – it's tailor-made. Why, these cuttings are even sponsored. Us punters are

corralled on the outside looking in. It may
come to pass that the meek shall inherit
the earth, but I prefer ostentation and
demonstration. So paint the roads with
cheap-shit slogans, though I could wish for
a graffiti styley of Francis Bacon's Screaming
Pope. Just as I love Brown Sugar but have
a sneakin' regard for Sugar Sugar by the
Archies when it pops up on the car radio.

Technology beckons – lasers triggered by
pressure pad contact with tyres, kinetic
installations featuring neon, and sound.
John Peel (RIP) always waxed lyrical about
a stretch of the M1 near Northampton which
had an experimental surface that made
ambient music as the wheels rolled over it.
He named it "The Orchestrated Highway".

I'm a sucker for the old ways, once so cutting-
edge. Vapour trail hearts ("I love Mario"),
prop-driven bi-planes towing banner messages
("I love Cipo"), slow boat traffic down the
holy Ganges, the ancient Nile, the mighty
Medway – forever vital, unpredictable,
uncontrollable. Soothing 'n' stimulating
simultaneously. Like Bobby Dylan, I'll just
sit here and watch the river flow.

Johnny Green

BEN INGHAM

"In Italy, for 30 years under the Borgias, they had warfare, terror, murder and bloodshed, but they produced Michelangelo, Leonardo da Vinci and the Renaissance. In Switzerland, they had brotherly love, they had 500 years of democracy and peace – and what did that produce? The cuckoo clock."
Orson Welles in The Third Man

It's the day before the Giro di Lombardia, and La Gazzetta dello Sport has just one page dedicated to the biggest one-day race on the Italian calendar. Qualifiers for football's World Cup rule the pink pages this October, even though the race is run by RCS, the Gazzetta-owned organisers of the Giro d'Italia. The Giro di Lombardia is but a sideshow.

It's no big surprise. After all, the world's dominant stadium sport is football, and the Italians love it as much as any other European nation. But the way sport is supported in each country is very different. One thing that strikes me, as a foreigner used to the vagaries of following the English game, is the singing on the Italian terraces. In Italy, they do it in grandstand-perfected unison which almost sounds orchestrated. It has to be heard to be believed. Cued in by a stadium announcer, the scene resembles a cathedral choir practice rather than hooligans jeering.

Sure, Italy has its share of problems with crowd violence, and the Ultras can be a pretty formidable bunch of head cases. But the tifosi are a generic group of sports fans that follows every sport from Formula 1 to cycling and from football to basketball, and for all their rowdiness, they are far more civilised than would first appear. Firstly, they make a day of it: families and friends attend in organised groups and eat at huge picnic tables – a contrast to the smaller, more intimate family scenes that take place on the roadside in France every summer, or the heaving mass in Belgian beer tents during spring. Secondly (and here's the big difference in Italian cycling culture), most of the fans aren't cyclists. In Britain, in America, in most "non-cycling" nations, almost all of the spectators are two-wheeled enthusiasts. But in Italy (and most of Europe's cycling heartlands for that matter) the crowds at the side of the road aren't exponents or enthusiasts. The fans are just that: fans.

At Lombardy we met one group of fans on the Passo del Ghisallo who had come from Bergamo to Como in a clapped-out school bus. They parked under a chestnut tree on the penultimate curve of the climb. Perfect. Once their fire was lit, barbecued liver delicately wrapped in prosciutto and hot roasted chestnuts from the tree were served. There is bread too and locally-made cheese, plus enough bottles of Barbera and home-brewed grappa to swill it all down. There is not a hotdog in sight, and they even had espresso. It's not really the feast you would expect outside Old Trafford or Stamford Bridge and it cost them just €15, including the minibus to the hill. The group of tifosi here certainly look like a football crowd – rough-faced men of all ages and tough-looking, they could easily be standing on the North Bank, the Shed End or the Spion Kop. The remarkable difference is the warm, inclusive and generous welcome. There's no bother here.

The wait for the main event is punctuated with local riders making their way up the hill. Cries of "Gimondi!" and "Coppi!" go out to those on Bianchis, and "Saronni!" to anyone on a red bike. As the race arrives, the grappa fuels screaming insults directed at the police until they sound their claxons – a response that is greeted with rapture. And then they start to sing. The songs are not of rivalry or hatred but love and sweethearts, harmonised and beautiful. Hooligans? No, not these tifosi.

After winning the 2006 World Cup, the streets of Rome, Milan and Turin echoed to The White Stripes' Seven Nations Army which, for some inexplicable reason, is the tifosi's current rabble-rousing song of choice. Perhaps it's just a tune well suited to impending action, or just a catchy anthem or fanfare. Today it is performed in unison, vigorously chanted as the helicopter hovers closer to the Ghisallo. The tifosi jump and wave, just as they would in the San Siro football stadium. The race whizzes by and Damiano Cunego smiles as he passes under the tree, dodging the drunken bodies. He didn't win. But it didn't matter.

Before football stadiums dominated the Italian city's sporting scene, there was the velodrome. The beautiful Fausto Coppi Velodrome on Corso Casale in Turin was the site of many grand finales (notably Milan-Turin, the oldest race on the cycling calendar) when cycling was the main stadium sport in towns across Italy. Now defunct but still a grand old building with steep concrete banks on the edge of a 391-metre track, it was the amphitheatre to the stars of post-war Italian cycling.

Years ago, the Giro often finished inside velodromes. If they arrived *gruppo compatto* at the gates of the velodrome, then the race would be stopped and the riders set off to time trial around the track. The grandstand finale would keep the audience captivated until the fastest lap was rewarded with the stage win. Herbie Sykes recalls one such night at Milan's track: "In the early evening of June 10th 1934, a massive crowd duly gathered at Milan's old velodrome as, one by one, the 52 survivors of the race concluded an 11-hour, 315km day in the saddle, with an insane 60-second thrash around the track. Meanwhile, in Rome, an even bigger multitude packed their sweaty bodies into the snappily-renamed Stadio Del Partita Nazionale Fascista, as Italy took on Czechoslovakians in the World Cup final. When the Milan stadium announcer broke the news that Italy had equalised ten minutes from time, the crowd, already in frenzy at the sight of Learco Guerra, Francesco Camusso and the like, went quite berserk. Then, at precisely the moment Giuseppe Olmo completed his maniacal, stage-winning 42-second lap, the announcer, peeing his metaphorical pants with excitement, deliriously let rip that Angelo Schiavio, Italian football's pin-up boy, had netted the winner. And off came the metaphorical roof..."

OK, so it's hardly in the realms of "those who are about to die salute you", but the comparisons with cycling and football are there and so are the comparisons with an older, more gruesome spectacle. A staggering statistic is that the Games in Rome went on at the Colosseum for 500 years, during which time half a million people were slaughtered and about twice as many animals were killed. The idea of it now is mind-boggling and horrific, but so is a Saturday afternoon down at Millwall FC. Sport has come a long way in Italy, and with it the supporters.

Long live the tifosi.

Guy Andrews

293

Image details